MAGIC

A FANTASTIC COMEDY

LSO BY G.K. CHESTERTON

The Defendant
Orthodoxy
Varied Types: Essays on Literature

MAGIC

A FANTASTIC COMEDY

BY

G.K. CHESTERTON

WILDSIDE PRESS

THE CHARACTERS

The Duke

Doctor Grimthorpe

The Rev. Cyril Smith

Morris Carleon

Hastings, the Duke's Secretary

The Stranger

Patricia Carleon

The action takes place in the Duke's Drawing-room.

NOTE

This play was presented under the management of Kenelm Foss at The Little Theatre, London, on November 7, 1913, with the following cast:

The Stranger: *Franklin Dyall*
Patricia Carleon: *Miss Grace Croft*
The Rev. Cyril Smith: *O.P. Heggie*
Dr. Grimthorpe: *William Farren*
The Duke: *Fred Lewis*
Hastings: *Frank Randell*
Morris Carleon: *Lyonel Watts*

THE PRELUDE

Scene: *A plantation of thin young trees, in a misty and rainy twilight; some woodland blossom showing the patches on the earth between the stems.*

The Stranger *is discovered, a cloaked figure with a pointed hood. His costume might belong to modern or any other time, and the conical hood is so drawn over the head that little can be seen of the face.*

A distant voice, a woman's, is heard, half-singing, half-chanting, unintelligible words. The cloaked figure raises its head and listens with interest. The song draws nearer and Patricia Carleon *enters. She is dark and slight, and has a dreamy expression. Though she is artistically dressed, her hair is a little wild. She has a broken branch of some flowering tree in her hand. She does not notice the stranger, and though he has watched her with interest, makes no sign. Suddenly she perceives him and starts back.*

PATRICIA. Oh! Who are you?

STRANGER. Ah! Who am I? [*Commences to mutter to himself, and maps out the ground with his staff.*]
 I have a hat, but not to wear;
 I wear a sword, but not to slay,
 And ever in my bag I bear
 A pack of cards, but not to play.

PATRICIA. What are you? What are you saying?

STRANGER. It is the language of the fairies, O daughter of Eve.

PATRICIA. But I never thought fairies were like you. Why, you are taller than I am.

STRANGER. We are of such stature as we will. But the elves grow small, not large, when they would mix with mortals.

PATRICIA. You mean they are beings greater than we are.

STRANGER. Daughter of men, if you would see a fairy as he truly is, look for his head above all the stars and his feet amid the floors of the sea. Old women have taught you that the fairies are too small to be seen. But I tell you the fairies are too mighty to be seen. For they are the elder gods before whom the giants were like pigmies. They are the Elemental Spirits, and any one of them is larger than the world. And you look for them in acorns and on toadstools and wonder that you never see them.

PATRICIA. But you come in the shape and size of a man?

STRANGER. Because I would speak with a woman.

PATRICIA. [*Drawing back in awe.*] I think you are growing taller as you speak.

[*The scene appears to fade away, and give place to the milieu of* Act One, *the Duke's drawing-room, an apartment with open French windows or any opening large enough to show a garden and one house fairly near. It is evening, and there is a red lamp lighted in the house beyond.* The Rev. Cyril Smith *is sitting with hat and umbrella beside him, evidently a visitor. He is a young man with the highest of High Church dog-collars and all the qualities of a restrained fanatic. He is one of*

*the Christian Socialist sort and takes his priesthood
seriously. He is an honest man, and not an ass.*

[*To him enters* Mr. Hastings *with papers in his
hand.*

HASTINGS. Oh, good evening. You are Mr. Smith.
[*Pause.*] I mean you are the Rector, I think.

SMITH. I am the Rector.

HASTINGS. I am the Duke's secretary. His Grace
asks me to say that he hopes to see you very soon; but
he is engaged just now with the Doctor.

SMITH. Is the Duke ill?

HASTINGS. [*Laughing.*] Oh, no; the Doctor has
come to ask him to help some cause or other. The Duke
is never ill.

SMITH. Is the Doctor with him now?

HASTINGS. Why, strictly speaking, he is not. The
Doctor has gone over the road to fetch a paper
connected with his proposal. But he hasn't far to go, as
you can see. That's his red lamp at the end of his
grounds.

SMITH. Yes, I know. I am much obliged to you. I
will wait as long as is necessary.

HASTINGS. [*Cheerfully.*] Oh, it won't be very
long.

[*Exit.*

[*Enter by the garden doors* Dr. Grimthorpe *reading
an open paper. He is an old-fashioned practitioner,
very much of a gentleman and very carefully dressed in
a slightly antiquated style. He is about sixty years old*

and might have been a friend of Huxley's.

DOCTOR. [*Folding up the paper.*] I beg your pardon, sir, I did not notice there was anyone here.

SMITH. [*Amicably.*] I beg yours. A new clergyman cannot expect to be expected. I only came to see the Duke about some local affairs.

DOCTOR. [*Smiling.*] And so, oddly enough, did I. But I suppose we should both like to get hold of him by a separate ear.

SMITH. Oh, there's no disguise as far as I'm concerned. I've joined this league for starting a model public-house in the parish; and in plain words, I've come to ask his Grace for a subscription to it.

DOCTOR. [*Grimly.*] And, as it happens, I have joined in the petition against the erection of a model public-house in this parish. The similarity of our position grows with every instant.

SMITH. Yes, I think we must have been twins.

DOCTOR. [*More good-humouredly.*] Well, what is a model public-house? Do you mean a toy?

SMITH. I mean a place where Englishmen can get decent drink and drink it decently. Do you call that a toy?

DOCTOR. No; I should call that a conjuring trick. Or, in apology to your cloth, I will say a miracle.

SMITH. I accept the apology to my cloth. I am doing my duty as a priest. How can the Church have a right to make men fast if she does not allow them to feast?

DOCTOR. [*Bitterly.*] And when you have done

feasting them, you will send them to me to be cured.

SMITH. Yes; and when you've done curing them you'll send them to me to be buried.

DOCTOR. [*After a pause, laughing.*] Well, you have all the old doctrines. It is only fair you should have all the old jokes too.

SMITH. [*Laughing also.*] By the way, you call it a conjuring trick that poor people should drink moderately.

DOCTOR. I call it a chemical discovery that alcohol is not a food.

SMITH. You don't drink wine yourself?

DOCTOR. [*Mildly startled.*] Drink wine! Well— what else is there to drink?

SMITH. So drinking decently is a conjuring trick that you can do, anyhow?

DOCTOR. [*Still good-humouredly.*] Well, well, let us hope so. Talking about conjuring tricks, there is to be conjuring and all kinds of things here this afternoon.

SMITH. Conjuring? Indeed? Why is that?

Enter Hastings *with a letter in each hand.*

HASTINGS. His Grace will be with you presently. He asked me to deal with the business matter first of all.

[*He gives a note to each of them.*

SMITH. [*Turning eagerly to the Doctor.*] But this is rather splendid. The Duke's given £50 to the new public-house.

HASTINGS. The Duke is very liberal.

[*Collects papers.*

DOCTOR. [*Examining his cheque.*] Very. But this is rather curious. He has also given £50 to the league for opposing the new public-house.

HASTINGS. The Duke is very liberal-minded.

[*Exit.*

SMITH. [*Staring at his cheque.*] Liberal-minded!... Absent-minded, I should call it.

DOCTOR. [*Sitting down and lighting a cigar.*] Well, yes. The Duke does suffer a little from absence [*puts his cigar in his mouth and pulls during the pause*] of mind. He is all for compromise. Don't you know the kind of man who, when you talk to him about the five best breeds of dog, always ends up by buying a mongrel? The Duke is the kindest of men, and always trying to please everybody. He generally finishes by pleasing nobody.

SMITH. Yes; I think I know the sort of thing.

DOCTOR. Take this conjuring, for instance. You know the Duke has two wards who are to live with him now?

SMITH. Yes. I heard something about a nephew and niece from Ireland.

DOCTOR. The niece came from Ireland some months ago, but the nephew comes back from America to-night. [*He gets up abruptly and walks about the room.*] I think I will tell you all about it. In spite of your precious public-house you seem to me to be a sane man. And I fancy I shall want all the sane men I can get to-night.

14

SMITH. [*Rising also.*] I am at your service. Do you know, I rather guessed you did not come here only to protest against my precious public-house.

DOCTOR. [*Striding about in subdued excitement.*] Well, you guessed right. I was family physician to the Duke's brother in Ireland. I knew the family pretty well.

SMITH. [*Quietly.*] I suppose you mean you knew something odd about the family?

DOCTOR. Well, they saw fairies and things of that sort.

SMITH. And I suppose, to the medical mind, seeing fairies means much the same as seeing snakes?

DOCTOR. [*With a sour smile.*] Well, they saw them in Ireland. I suppose it's quite correct to see fairies in Ireland. It's like gambling at Monte Carlo. It's quite respectable. But I do draw the line at their seeing fairies in England. I do object to their bringing their ghosts and goblins and witches into the poor Duke's own back garden and within a yard of my own red lamp. It shows a lack of tact.

SMITH. But I do understand that the Duke's nephew and niece see witches and fairies between here and your lamp.

[*He walks to the garden window and looks out.*

DOCTOR. Well, the nephew has been in America. It stands to reason you can't see fairies in America. But there is this sort of superstition in the family, and I am not easy in my mind about the girl.

SMITH. Why, what does she do?

DOCTOR. Oh, she wanders about the park and the woods in the evenings. Damp evenings for choice. She calls it the Celtic twilight. I've no use for the Celtic twilight myself. It has a tendency to get on the chest. But what is worse, she is always talking about meeting somebody, some elf or wizard or something. I don't like it at all.

SMITH. Have you told the Duke?

DOCTOR. [*With a grim smile.*] Oh, yes, I told the Duke. The result was the conjurer.

SMITH. [*With amazement.*] The conjurer?

DOCTOR. [*Puts down his cigar in the ash-tray.*] The Duke is indescribable. He will be here presently, and you shall judge for yourself. Put two or three facts or ideas before him, and the thing he makes out of them is always something that seems to have nothing to do with it. Tell any other human being about a girl dreaming of the fairies and her practical brother from America, and he would settle it in some obvious way and satisfy some one: send her to America or let her have her fairies in Ireland. Now the Duke thinks a conjurer would just meet the case. I suppose he vaguely thinks it would brighten things up, and somehow satisfy the believers' interest in supernatural things and the unbelievers' interest in smart things. As a matter of fact the unbeliever thinks the conjurer's a fraud, and the believer thinks he's a fraud, too. The conjurer satisfies nobody. That is why he satisfies the Duke.

[*Enter the* Duke, *with* Hastings, *carrying papers. The Duke is a healthy, hearty man in tweeds, with a rather wandering eye. In the present state of the peerage it is necessary to explain that the* Duke, *though an ass, is a gentleman.*

16

DUKE. Good-morning, Mr. Smith. So sorry to have kept you waiting, but we're rather in a rush to-day. [*Turns to* Hastings, *who has gone over to a table with the papers.*] You know Mr. Carleon is coming this afternoon?

HASTINGS. Yes, your Grace. His train will be in by now. I have sent the trap.

DUKE. Thank you. [*Turning to the other two.*] My nephew, Dr. Grimthorpe, Morris, you know, Miss Carleon's brother from America. I hear he's been doing great things out there. Petrol, or something. Must move with the times, eh?

DOCTOR. I'm afraid Mr. Smith doesn't always agree with moving with the times.

DUKE. Oh, come, come! Progress, you know, progress! Of course I know how busy you are; you mustn't overwork yourself, you know. Hastings was telling me you laughed over those subscriptions of mine. Well, well, I believe in looking at both sides of a question, you know. Aspects, as old Buffle called them. Aspects. [*With an all-embracing gesture of the arm.*] You represent the tendency to drink in moderation, and you do good in your way. The Doctor represents the tendency not to drink at all; and he does good in his way. We can't be Ancient Britons, you know.

[*A prolonged and puzzled silence, such as always follows the more abrupt of the* Duke's *associations or disassociations of thought.*

SMITH. [*At last, faintly.*] Ancient Britons....

DOCTOR. [*To* Smith *in a low voice.*] Don't bother. It's only his broad-mindedness.

17

DUKE. [*With unabated cheerfulness.*] I saw the place you're putting up for it, Mr. Smith. Very good work. Very good work, indeed. Art for the people, eh? I particularly liked that woodwork over the west door— I'm glad to see you're using the new sort of graining ... why, it all reminds one of the French Revolution.

[*Another silence. As the* Duke *lounges alertly about the room,* Smith *speaks to the* Doctor *in an undertone.*

SMITH. Does it remind you of the French Revolution?

DOCTOR. As much as of anything else. His Grace never reminds me of anything.

[*A young and very high American voice is heard calling in the garden. "Say, could somebody see to one of these trunks?"*

[Mr. Hastings *goes out into the garden. He returns with* Morris Carleon, *a very young man: hardly more than a boy, but with very grown-up American dress and manners. He is dark, smallish, and active; and the racial type under his Americanism is Irish.*

MORRIS. [*Humorously, as he puts in his head at the window.*] See here, does a Duke live here?

DOCTOR. [*Who is nearest to him, with great gravity.*] Yes, only one.

MORRIS. I reckon he's the one I want, anyhow. I'm his nephew.

[*The* Duke, *who is ruminating in the foreground, with one eye rather off, turns at the voice and shakes* Morris *warmly by the hand.*

DUKE. Delighted to see you, my dear boy. I hear

18

you've been doing very well for yourself.

MORRIS. [*Laughing.*] Well, pretty well, Duke; and better still for Paul T. Vandam, I guess. I manage the old man's mines out in Arizona, you know.

DUKE. [*Shaking his head sagaciously.*] Ah, very go-ahead man! Very go-ahead methods, I'm told. Well, I dare say he does a great deal of good with his money. And we can't go back to the Spanish Inquisition.

[*Silence, during which the three men look at each other.*

MORRIS. [*Abruptly.*] And how's Patricia?

DUKE. [*A little hazily.*] Oh, she's very well, I think. She....

[*He hesitates slightly.*

MORRIS. [*Smiling.*] Well, then, where's Patricia?

[*There is a slightly embarrassed pause, and the Doctor speaks.*

DOCTOR. Miss Carleon is walking about the grounds, I think.

[Morris *goes to the garden doors and looks out.*

MORRIS. It's a mighty chilly night to choose. Does my sister commonly select such evenings to take the air—and the damp?

DOCTOR. [*After a pause.*] If I may say so, I quite agree with you. I have often taken the liberty of warning your sister against going out in all weathers like this.

DUKE. [*Expansively waving his hands about.*] The artist temperament! What I always call the artistic temperament! Wordsworth, you know, and all that.

[*Silence.*

MORRIS. [*Staring.*] All what?

DUKE. [*Continuing to lecture with enthusiasm.*] Why, everything's temperament, you know! It's her temperament to see the fairies. It's my temperament not to see the fairies. Why, I've walked all round the grounds twenty times and never saw a fairy. Well, it's like that about this wizard or whatever she calls it. For her there is somebody there. For us there would not be somebody there. Don't you see?

MORRIS. [*Advancing excitedly.*] Somebody there! What do you mean?

DUKE. [*Airily.*] Well, you can't quite call it a man.

MORRIS. [*Violently.*] A man!

DUKE. Well, as old Buffle used to say, what is a man?

MORRIS. [*With a strong rise of the American accent.*] With your permission, Duke, I eliminate old Buffle. Do you mean that anybody has had the tarnation coolness to suggest that some man....

DUKE. Oh, not a man, you know. A magician, something mythical, you know.

SMITH. Not a man, but a medicine man.

DOCTOR. [*Grimly.*] I am a medicine man.

MORRIS. And you don't look mythical, Doc.

[*He bites his finger and begins to pace restlessly up and down the room.*

DUKE. Well, you know, the artistic temperament....

MORRIS. [*Turning suddenly.*] See here, Duke! In most commercial ways we're a pretty forward country. In these moral ways we're content to be a pretty backward country. And if you ask me whether I like my sister walking about the woods on a night like this! Well, I don't.

DUKE. I am afraid you Americans aren't so advanced as I'd hoped. Why! as old Buffle used to say....

[*As he speaks a distant voice is heard singing in the garden; it comes nearer and nearer, and* Smith *turns suddenly to the* Doctor.

SMITH. Whose voice is that?

DOCTOR. It is no business of mine to decide!

MORRIS. [*Walking to the window.*] You need not trouble. I know who it is.

[*Enter* Patricia Carleon

[*Still agitated.*] Patricia, where have you been?

PATRICIA. [*Rather wearily.*] Oh! in Fairyland.

DOCTOR. [*Genially.*] And whereabouts is that?

PATRICIA. It's rather different from other places. It's either nowhere or it's wherever you are.

MORRIS. [*Sharply.*] Has it any inhabitants?

PATRICIA. Generally only two. Oneself and one's shadow. But whether he is my shadow or I am his shadow is never found out.

MORRIS. He? Who?

PATRICIA. [*Seeming to understand his annoyance for the first time, and smiling.*] Oh, you needn't get

21

conventional about it, Morris. He is not a mortal.

MORRIS. What's his name?

PATRICIA. We have no names there. You never really know anybody if you know his name.

MORRIS. What does he look like?

PATRICIA. I have only met him in the twilight. He seems robed in a long cloak, with a peaked cap or hood like the elves in my nursery stories. Sometimes when I look out of the window here, I see him passing round this house like a shadow; and see his pointed hood, dark against the sunset or the rising of the moon.

SMITH. What does he talk about?

PATRICIA. He tells me the truth. Very many true things. He is a wizard.

MORRIS. How do you know he's a wizard? I suppose he plays some tricks on you.

PATRICIA. I should know he was a wizard if he played no tricks. But once he stooped and picked up a stone and cast it into the air, and it flew up into God's heaven like a bird.

MORRIS. Was that what first made you think he was a wizard?

PATRICIA. Oh, no. When I first saw him he was tracing circles and pentacles in the grass and talking the language of the elves.

MORRIS. [Sceptically.] Do you know the language of the elves?

PATRICIA. Not until I heard it.

MORRIS. [Lowering his voice as if for his sister,

but losing patience so completely that he talks much louder than he imagines.] See here, Patricia, I reckon this kind of thing is going to be the limit. I'm just not going to have you let in by some blamed tramp or fortune-teller because you choose to read minor poetry about the fairies. If this gipsy or whatever he is troubles you again....

DOCTOR. [*Putting his hand on* Morris's *shoulder.*] Come, you must allow a little more for poetry. We can't all feed on nothing but petrol.

DUKE. Quite right, quite right. And being Irish, don't you know, Celtic, as old Buffle used to say, charming songs, you know, about the Irish girl who has a plaid shawl—and a Banshee. [*Sighs profoundly.*] Poor old Gladstone!

[*Silence as usual.*

SMITH. [*Speaking to* Doctor.] I thought you yourself considered the family superstition bad for the health?

DOCTOR. I consider a family superstition is better for the health than a family quarrel. [*He walks casually across to* Patricia.] Well, it must be nice to be young and still see all those stars and sunsets. We old buffers won't be too strict with you if your view of things sometimes gets a bit—mixed up, shall we say? If the stars get loose about the grass by mistake; or if, once or twice, the sunset gets into the east. We should only say, "Dream as much as you like. Dream for all mankind. Dream for us who can dream no longer. But do not quite forget the difference."

PATRICIA. What difference?

DOCTOR. The difference between the things that

23

are beautiful and the things that are there. That red lamp over my door isn't beautiful; but it's there. You might even come to be glad it is there, when the stars of gold and silver have faded. I am an old man now, but some men are still glad to find my red star. I do not say they are the wise men.

PATRICIA. [*Somewhat affected.*] Yes, I know you are good to everybody. But don't you think there may be floating and spiritual stars which will last longer than the red lamps?

SMITH. [*With decision.*] Yes. But they are fixed stars.

DOCTOR. The red lamp will last my time.

DUKE. Capital! Capital! Why, it's like Tennyson. [*Silence.*] I remember when I was an undergrad....

[*The red light disappears; no one sees it at first except* Patricia, *who points excitedly.*

MORRIS. What's the matter?

PATRICIA. The red star is gone.

MORRIS. Nonsense! [*Rushes to the garden doors.*] It's only somebody standing in front of it. Say, Duke, there's somebody standing in the garden.

PATRICIA. [*Calmly.*] I told you he walked about the garden.

MORRIS. If it's that fortune-teller of yours....

[*Disappears into the garden, followed by the* Doctor.

DUKE. [*Staring.*] Somebody in the garden! Really, this Land Campaign....

[*Silence.*

[Morris *reappears rather breathless.*

MORRIS. A spry fellow, your friend. He slipped through my hands like a shadow.

PATRICIA. I told you he was a shadow.

MORRIS. Well, I guess there's going to be a shadow hunt. Got a lantern, Duke?

PATRICIA. Oh, you need not trouble. He will come if I call him.

[*She goes out into the garden and calls out some half-chanted and unintelligible words, somewhat like the song preceding her entrance. The red light reappears; and there is a slight sound as of fallen leaves shuffled by approaching feet. The cloaked* Stranger *with the pointed hood is seen standing outside the garden doors.*

PATRICIA. You may enter all doors.

[*The figure comes into the room*

MORRIS. [*Shutting the garden doors behind him.*] Now, see here, wizard, we've got you. And we know you're a fraud.

SMITH. [*Quietly.*] Pardon me, I do not fancy that we know that. For myself I must confess to something of the Doctor's agnosticism.

MORRIS. [*Excited, and turning almost with a snarl.*] I didn't know you parsons stuck up for any fables but your own.

SMITH. I stick up for the thing every man has a right to. Perhaps the only thing that every man has a

25

right to.

MORRIS. And what is that?

SMITH. The benefit of the doubt. Even your master, the petroleum millionaire, has a right to that. And I think he needs it more.

MORRIS. I don't think there's much doubt about the question, Minister. I've met this sort of fellow often enough—the sort of fellow who wheedles money out of girls by telling them he can make stones disappear.

DOCTOR. [*To the* Stranger.] Do you say you can make stones disappear?

STRANGER. Yes. I can make stones disappear.

MORRIS. [*Roughly.*] I reckon you're the kind of tough who knows how to make a watch and chain disappear.

STRANGER. Yes; I know how to make a watch and chain disappear.

MORRIS. And I should think you were pretty good at disappearing yourself.

STRANGER. I have done such a thing.

MORRIS. [*With a sneer.*] Will you disappear now?

STRANGER. [*After reflection.*] No, I think I'll appear instead. [*He throws back his hood, showing the head of an intellectual-looking man, young but rather worn. Then he unfastens his cloak and throws it off, emerging in complete modern evening dress. He advances down the room towards the* Duke, *taking out his watch as he does so.*] Good-evening, your Grace. I'm afraid I'm rather too early for the performance. But this gentleman [*with a gesture towards* Morris] seemed rather impatient for it to begin.

DUKE. [*Rather at a loss.*] Oh, good-evening. Why, really—are you the...?

STRANGER. [*Bowing.*] Yes. I am the Conjurer.

[*There is general laughter, except from* Patricia. *As the others mingle in talk, the* Stranger *goes up to her.*

STRANGER. [*Very sadly.*] I am very sorry I am not a wizard.

PATRICIA. I wish you were a thief instead.

STRANGER. Have I committed a worse crime than thieving?

PATRICIA. You have committed the cruellest crime, I think, that there is.

STRANGER. And what is the cruellest crime?

PATRICIA. Stealing a child's toy.

STRANGER. And what have I stolen?

PATRICIA. A fairy tale.

CURTAIN

ACT II

The same room lighted more brilliantly an hour later in the evening. On one side a table covered with packs of cards, pyramids, etc., at which the Conjurer in evening dress is standing quietly setting out his tricks. A little more in the foreground the Duke; and Hastings with a number of papers.

HASTINGS. There are only a few small matters. Here are the programmes of the entertainment your Grace wanted. Mr. Carleon wishes to see them very much.

DUKE. Thanks, thanks. [*Takes the programmes.*]

HASTINGS. Shall I carry them for your Grace?

DUKE. No, no; I shan't forget, I shan't forget. Why, you've no idea how businesslike I am. We have to be, you know. [*Vaguely.*] I know you're a bit of a Socialist; but I assure you there's a good deal to do— stake in the country, and all that. Look at remembering faces now! The King never forgets faces. [*Waves the programmes about.*] I never forget faces. [*Catches sight of the* Conjurer *and genially draws him into the discussion.*] Why, the Professor here who performs before the King [*puts down the programmes*]—you see it on the caravans, you know—performs before the King almost every night, I suppose....

CONJURER. [*Smiling.*] I sometimes let his Majesty have an evening off. And turn my attention, of course, to the very highest nobility. But naturally I have performed before every sovereign potentate, white and black. There never was a conjurer who hadn't.

DUKE. That's right, that's right! And you'll say with me that the great business for a King is remembering people?

CONJURER. I should say it was remembering which people to remember.

DUKE. Well, well, now.... [*Looks round rather wildly for something.*] Being really businesslike....

HASTINGS. Shall I take the programmes for your Grace?

DUKE. [*Picking them up.*] No, no, I shan't forget. Is there anything else?

HASTINGS. I have to go down the village about the wire to Stratford. The only other thing at all urgent is the Militant Vegetarians.

DUKE. Ah! The Militant Vegetarians! You've heard of them, I'm sure. Won't obey the law [*to the* Conjurer] so long as the Government serves out meat.

CONJURER. Let them be comforted. There are a good many people who don't get much meat.

DUKE. Well, well, I'm bound to say they're very enthusiastic. Advanced, too—oh, certainly advanced. Like Joan of Arc.

[*Short silence, in which the* Conjurer *stares at him.*]

CONJURER. Was Joan of Arc a Vegetarian?

DUKE. Oh, well, it's a very high ideal, after all. The Sacredness of Life, you know—the Sacredness of Life. [*Shakes his head.*] But they carry it too far. They killed a policeman down in Kent.

CONJURER. Killed a policeman? How Vegetarian!

Well, I suppose it was, so long as they didn't eat him.

HASTINGS. They are asking only for small subscriptions. Indeed, they prefer to collect a large number of half-crowns, to prove the popularity of their movement. But I should advise....

DUKE. Oh, give them three shillings, then.

HASTINGS. If I might suggest....

DUKE. Hang it all! We gave the Anti-Vegetarians three shillings. It seems only fair.

HASTINGS. If I might suggest anything, I think your Grace will be wise not to subscribe in this case. The Anti-Vegetarians have already used their funds to form gangs ostensibly to protect their own meetings. And if the Vegetarians use theirs to break up the meetings—well, it will look rather funny that we have paid roughs on both sides. It will be rather difficult to explain when it comes before the magistrate.

DUKE. But I shall be the magistrate. [Conjurer *stares at him again*.] That's the system, my dear Hastings, that's the advantage of the system. Not a logical system—no Rousseau in it—but see how well it works! I shall be the very best magistrate that could be on the Bench. The others would be biassed, you know. Old Sir Lawrence is a Vegetarian himself; and might be hard on the Anti-Vegetarian roughs. Colonel Crashaw would be sure to be hard on the Vegetarian roughs. But if I've paid both of 'em, of course I shan't be hard on either of 'em—and there you have it. Just perfect impartiality.

HASTINGS. [*Restrainedly*.] Shall I take the programmes, your Grace?

DUKE. [*Heartily.*] No, no; I won't forget 'em. [*Exit* Hastings.] Well, Professor, what's the news in the conjuring world?

CONJURER. I fear there is never any news in the conjuring world.

DUKE. Don't you have a newspaper or something? Everybody has a newspaper now, you know. The—er— Daily Sword-Swallower or that sort of thing?

CONJURER. No, I have been a journalist myself; but I think journalism and conjuring will always be incompatible.

DUKE. Incompatible—Oh, but that's where I differ—that's where I take larger views! Larger laws, as old Buffle said. Nothing's incompatible, you know— except husband and wife and so on; you must talk to Morris about that. It's wonderful the way incompatibility has gone forward in the States.

CONJURER. I only mean that the two trades rest on opposite principles. The whole point of being a conjurer is that you won't explain a thing that has happened.

DUKE. Well, and the journalist?

CONJURER. Well, the whole point of being a journalist is that you do explain a thing that hasn't happened.

DUKE. But you'll want somewhere to discuss the new tricks.

CONJURER. There are no new tricks. And if there were we shouldn't want 'em discussed.

DUKE. I'm afraid you're not really advanced. Are you interested in modern progress?

CONJURER. Yes. We are interested in all tricks done by illusion.

DUKE. Well, well, I must go and see how Morris is. Pleasure of seeing you later.

[*Exit* Duke, *leaving the programmes.*

CONJURER. Why are nice men such asses? [*Turns to arrange the table.*] That seems all right. The pack of cards that is a pack of cards. And the pack of cards that isn't a pack of cards. The hat that looks like a gentleman's hat. But which, in reality, is no gentleman's hat. Only my hat; and I am not a gentleman. I am only a conjurer, and this is only a conjurer's hat. I could not take off this hat to a lady. I can take rabbits out of it, goldfish out of it, snakes out of it. Only I mustn't take my own head out of it. I suppose I'm a lower animal than a rabbit or a snake. Anyhow they can get out of the conjurer's hat; and I can't. I am a conjurer and nothing else but a conjurer. Unless I could show I was something else, and that would be worse.

[*He begins to dash the cards rather irregularly about the table. Enter* Patricia.

PATRICIA. [*Coldly*] I beg your pardon. I came to get some programmes. My uncle wants them.

[*She walks swiftly across and takes up the programmes.*

CONJURER. [*Still dashing cards about the table.*] Miss Carleon, might I speak to you a moment? [*He puts his hands in his pockets, stares at the table; and his face assumes a sardonic expression.*] The question is purely practical.

PATRICIA. [*Pausing at the door.*] I can hardly imagine what the question can be.

CONJURER. I am the question.

PATRICIA. And what have I to do with that?

CONJURER. You have everything to do with it. I am the question: you....

PATRICIA. [*Angrily.*] Well, what am I?

CONJURER. You are the answer.

PATRICIA. The answer to what?

CONJURER. [*Coming round to the front of the table and sitting against it.*] The answer to me. You think I'm a liar because I walked about the fields with you and said I could make stones disappear. Well, so I can. I'm a conjurer. In mere point of fact, it wasn't a lie. But if it had been a lie I should have told it just the same. I would have told twenty such lies. You may or may not know why.

PATRICIA. I know nothing about such lies.

[*She puts her hand on the handle of the door, but the* Conjurer, *who is sitting on the table and staring at his boots, does not notice the action, and goes on as in a sincere soliloquy.*

CONJURER. I don't know whether you have any notion of what it means to a man like me to talk to a lady like you, even on false pretences. I am an adventurer. I am a blackguard, if one can earn the title by being in all the blackguard societies of the world. I have thought everything out by myself, when I was a guttersnipe in Fleet Street, or, lower still, a journalist in Fleet Street. Before I met you I never guessed that rich people ever thought at all. Well, that is all I have to say. We had some good conversations, didn't we? I am a liar. But I told you a great deal of the truth.

[*He turns and resumes the arrangement of the table.*

PATRICIA. [*Thinking.*] Yes, you did tell me a great deal of the truth. You told me hundreds and thousands of truths. But you never told me the truth that one wants to know.

CONJURER. And what is that?

PATRICIA. [*Turning back into the room.*] You never told me the truth about yourself. You never told me you were only the Conjurer.

CONJURER. I did not tell you that because I do not even know it. I do not know whether I am only the Conjurer....

PATRICIA. What do you mean?

CONJURER. Sometimes I am afraid I am something worse than the Conjurer.

PATRICIA. [*Seriously.*] I cannot think of anything worse than a conjurer who does not call himself a conjurer.

CONJURER. [*Gloomily.*] There is something worse. [*Rallying himself.*] But that is not what I want to say. Do you really find that very unpardonable? Come, let me put you a case. Never mind about whether it is our case. A man spends his time incessantly in going about in third-class carriages to fifth-rate lodgings. He has to make up new tricks, new patter, new nonsense, sometimes every night of his life. Mostly he has to do it in the beastly black cities of the Midlands and the North, where he can't get out into the country. Now and again he does it at some gentleman's country-house, where he can get out into the country. Well, you know that actors and orators and all sorts of people like to rehearse their effects in the open air if they can. [*Smiles.*] You know that story of the great statesman who was heard by his own gardener saying, as he paced the garden, "Had I, Mr. Speaker, received the smallest intimation that I could be called upon to speak this evening...." [Patricia *controls a smile, and he goes on with overwhelming enthusiasm.*] Well, conjurers are just the same. It takes some time to prepare an impromptu. A man like that walks about the woods and fields doing all his tricks beforehand, and talking all sorts of gibberish because he thinks he is alone. One evening this man found he was not alone. He found a very beautiful child was watching him.

PATRICIA. A child?

CONJURER. Yes. That was his first impression. He is an intimate friend of mine. I have known him all my life. He tells me he has since discovered she is not a child. She does not fulfil the definition.

PATRICIA. What is the definition of a child?

CONJURER. Somebody you can play with.

PATRICIA. [*Abruptly.*] Why did you wear that cloak with the hood up?

CONJURER. [*Smiling.*] I think it escaped your notice that it was raining.

PATRICIA. [*Smiling faintly.*] And what did this friend of yours do?

CONJURER. You have already told me what he did. He destroyed a fairy tale, for he created a fairy tale that he was bound to destroy. [*Swinging round suddenly on the table.*] But do you blame a man very much, Miss Carleon, if he enjoyed the only fairy tale he had had in his life? Suppose he said the silly circles he was drawing for practice were really magic circles? Suppose he said the bosh he was talking was the language of the elves? Remember, he has read fairy tales as much as you have. Fairy tales are the only democratic institutions. All the classes have heard all the fairy tales. Do you blame him very much if he, too, tried to have a holiday in fairyland?

PATRICIA. [*Simply.*] I blame him less than I did. But I still say there can be nothing worse than false magic. And, after all, it was he who brought the false magic.

CONJURER. [*Rising from his seat.*] Yes. It was she who brought the real magic.

[*Enter* Morris, *in evening-dress. He walks straight up to the conjuring-table; and picks up one article after another, putting each down with a comment.*

MORRIS. I know that one. I know that. I know that. Let's see, that's the false bottom, I think. That works with a wire. I know that; it goes up the sleeve. That's the false bottom again. That's the substituted pack of cards—that....

PATRICIA. Really, Morris, you mustn't talk as if you knew everything.

CONJURER. Oh, I don't mind anyone knowing everything, Miss Carleon. There is something that is much more important than knowing how a thing is done.

MORRIS. And what's that?

CONJURER. Knowing how to do it.

MORRIS. [*Becoming nasal again in anger.*] That's so, eh? Being the high-toned conjurer because you can't any longer take all the sidewalk as a fairy.

PATRICIA. [*Crossing the room and speaking seriously to her brother.*] Really, Morris, you are very rude. And it's quite ridiculous to be rude. This gentleman was only practising some tricks by himself in the garden. [*With a certain dignity.*] If there was any mistake, it was mine. Come, shake hands, or whatever men do when they apologize. Don't be silly. He won't turn you into a bowl of goldfish.

MORRIS. [*Reluctantly.*] Well, I guess that's so. [*Offering his hand.*] Shake. [*They shake hands.*] And you won't turn me into a bowl of goldfish anyhow, Professor. I understand that when you do produce a bowl of goldfish, they are generally slips of carrot. That is so, Professor?

CONJURER. [*Sharply.*] Yes. [*Produces a bowl of goldfish from his tail pockets and holds it under the other's nose.*] Judge for yourself.

MORRIS. [*In monstrous excitement.*] Very good! Very good! But I know how that's done—I know how that's done. You have an india-rubber cap, you know, or cover....

CONJURER. Yes.

[*Goes back gloomily to his table and sits on it, picking up a pack of cards and balancing it in his hand.*

MORRIS. Ah, most mysteries are tolerably plain if you know the apparatus. [*Enter* Doctor *and* Smith, *talking with grave faces, but growing silent as they reach the group.*] I guess I wish we had all the old apparatus of all the old Priests and Prophets since the beginning of the world. I guess most of the old miracles and that were a matter of just panel and wires.

CONJURER. I don't quite understand you. What old apparatus do you want so much?

MORRIS. [*Breaking out with all the frenzy of the young free-thinker.*] Well, sir, I just want that old apparatus that turned rods into snakes. I want those smart appliances, sir, that brought water out of a rock when old man Moses chose to hit it. I guess it's a pity we've lost the machinery. I would like to have those old conjurers here that called themselves Patriarchs and Prophets in your precious Bible....

PATRICIA. Morris, you mustn't talk like that.

MORRIS. Well, I don't believe in religion....

DOCTOR. [*Aside.*] Hush, hush. Nobody but women believe in religion.

PATRICIA. [*Humorously.*] I think this is a fitting opportunity to show you another ancient conjuring trick.

DOCTOR. Which one is that?

PATRICIA. The Vanishing Lady!

[*Exit Patricia.*

SMITH. There is one part of their old apparatus I regret especially being lost.

MORRIS. [*Still excited.*] Yes!

SMITH. The apparatus for writing the Book of Job.

MORRIS. Well, well, they didn't know everything

in those old times.

SMITH. No, and in those old times they knew they didn't. [*Dreamily.*] Where shall wisdom be found, and what is the place of understanding?

CONJURER. Somewhere in America, I believe.

SMITH. [*Still dreamily.*] Man knoweth not the price thereof; neither is it found in the land of the living. The deep sayeth it is not in me, the sea sayeth it is not with me. Death and destruction say we have heard tell of it. God understandeth the way thereof and He knoweth the place thereof. For He looketh to the ends of the earth and seeth under the whole Heaven. But to man He hath said: Behold the fear of the Lord that is wisdom, and to depart from evil is understanding. [*Turns suddenly to the* Doctor.] How's that for Agnosticism, Dr. Grimthorpe? What a pity that apparatus is lost.

MORRIS. Well, you may just smile how you choose, I reckon. But I say the Conjurer here could be the biggest man in the big blessed centuries if he could just show us how the Holy old tricks were done. We must say this for old man Moses, that he was in advance of his time. When he did the old tricks they were new tricks. He got the pull on the public. He could do his tricks before grown men, great bearded fighting men who could win battles and sing Psalms. But this modern conjuring is all behind the times. That's why they only do it with schoolboys. There isn't a trick on that table I don't know. The whole trade's as dead as mutton; and not half so satisfying. Why he [*pointing to the* Conjurer] brought out a bowl of goldfish just now— an old trick that anybody could do.

CONJURER. Oh, I quite agree. The apparatus is perfectly simple. By the way, let me have a look at those goldfish of yours, will you?

MORRIS. [*Angrily.*] I'm not a paid play-actor come here to conjure. I'm not here to do stale tricks; I'm here to see through 'em. I say it's an old trick and....

CONJURER. True. But as you said, we never show it except to schoolboys.

MORRIS. And may I ask you, Professor Hocus Pocus, or whatever your name is, whom you are calling a schoolboy?

CONJURER. I beg your pardon. Your sister will tell you I am sometimes mistaken about children.

MORRIS. I forbid you to appeal to my sister.

CONJURER. That is exactly what a schoolboy would do.

MORRIS. [*With abrupt and dangerous calm.*] I am not a schoolboy, Professor. I am a quiet business man. But I tell you in the country I come from, the hand of a quiet business man goes to his hip pocket at an insult like that.

CONJURER. [*Fiercely.*] Let it go to his pocket! I thought the hand of a quiet business man more often went to someone else's pocket.

MORRIS. You....

[*Puts his hand to his hip. The* Doctor *puts his hand on his shoulder.*

DOCTOR. Gentlemen, I think you are both forgetting yourselves.

CONJURER. Perhaps. [*His tone sinks suddenly to weariness.*] I ask pardon for what I said. It was certainly

41

in excess of the young gentleman's deserts. [*Sighs.*] I sometimes rather wish I could forget myself.

MORRIS. [*Sullenly, after a pause.*] Well, the entertainment's coming on; and you English don't like a scene. I reckon I'll have to bury the blamed old hatchet too.

DOCTOR. [*With a certain dignity, his social type shining through his profession.*] Mr. Carleon, you will forgive an old man, who knew your father well, if he doubts whether you are doing yourself justice in treating yourself as an American Indian, merely because you have lived in America. In my old friend Huxley's time we of the middle classes disbelieved in reason and all sorts of things. But we did believe in good manners. It is a pity if the aristocracy can't. I don't like to hear you say you are a savage and have buried a tomahawk. I would rather hear you say, as your Irish ancestors would have said, that you have sheathed your sword with the dignity proper to a gentleman.

MORRIS. Very well. I've sheathed my sword with the dignity proper to a gentleman.

CONJURER. And I have sheathed my sword with the dignity proper to a conjurer.

MORRIS. How does the Conjurer sheath a sword?

CONJURER. Swallows it.

DOCTOR. Then we all agree there shall be no quarrel.

SMITH. May I say a word? I have a great dislike of a quarrel, for a reason quite beyond my duty to my cloth.

MORRIS. And what is that?

SMITH. I object to a quarrel because it always interrupts an argument. May I bring you back for a moment to the argument? You were saying that these modern conjuring tricks are simply the old miracles when they have once been found out. But surely another view is possible. When we speak of things being sham, we generally mean that they are imitations of things that are genuine. Take that Reynolds over there of the Duke's great-grandfather. [*Points to a picture on the wall.*] If I were to say it was a copy....

MORRIS. Wal, the Duke's real amiable; but I reckon you'd find what you call the interruption of an argument.

SMITH. Well, suppose I did say so, you wouldn't take it as meaning that Sir Joshua Reynolds never lived. Why should sham miracles prove to us that real Saints and Prophets never lived. There may be sham magic and real magic also.

[*The* Conjurer *raises his head and listens with a strange air of intentness.*

SMITH. There may be turnip ghosts precisely because there are real ghosts. There may be theatrical fairies precisely because there are real fairies. You do not abolish the Bank of England by pointing to a forged bank-note.

MORRIS. I hope the Professor enjoys being called a forged bank-note.

CONJURER. Almost as much as being called the Prospectus of some American Companies.

DOCTOR. Gentlemen! Gentlemen!

CONJURER. I am sorry.

MORRIS. Wal, let's have the argument first, then I guess we can have the quarrel afterwards. I'll clean this house of some encumbrances. See here, Mr. Smith, I'm not putting anything on your real miracle notion. I say, and Science says, that there's a cause for everything. Science will find out that cause, and sooner or later your old miracle will look mighty mean. Sooner or later Science will botanise a bit on your turnip ghosts; and make you look turnips yourselves for having taken any. I say....

DOCTOR. [*In a low voice to Smith.*] I don't like this peaceful argument of yours. The boy is getting much too excited.

MORRIS. You say old man Reynolds lived; and Science don't say no. [*He turns excitedly to the picture.*] But I guess he's dead now; and you'll no more raise your Saints and Prophets from the dead than you'll raise the Duke's great-grandfather to dance on that wall.

[*The picture begins to sway slightly to and fro on the wall.*

DOCTOR. Why, the picture is moving!

MORRIS. [*Turning furiously on the* Conjurer.] You were in the room before us. Do you reckon that will take us in? You can do all that with wires.

CONJURER. [*Motionless and without looking up from the table.*] Yes, I could do all that with wires.

MORRIS. And you reckoned I shouldn't know. [*Laughs with a high crowing laugh.*] That's how the derned dirty Spiritualists do all their tricks. They say they can make the furniture move of itself. If it does move they move it; and we mean to know how.

[*A chair falls over with a slight crash.*

[Morris *almost staggers and momentarily fights for breath and words.*

MORRIS. You ... why ... that ... every one knows that ... a sliding plank. It can be done with a sliding plank.

CONJURER. [*Without looking up.*] Yes. It can be done with a sliding plank.

[*The* Doctor *draws nearer to* Morris, *who faces about, addressing him passionately.*

MORRIS. You were right on the spot, Doc, when you talked about that red lamp of yours. That red lamp is the light of science that will put out all the lanterns of your turnip ghosts. It's a consuming fire, Doctor, but it is the red light of the morning. [*Points at it in exalted enthusiasm.*] Your priests can no more stop that light from shining or change its colour and its radiance than Joshua could stop the sun and moon. [*Laughs savagely.*] Why, a real fairy in an elfin cloak strayed too near the lamp an hour or two ago; and it turned him into a common society clown with a white tie.

[*The lamp at the end of the garden turns blue. They all look at it in silence.*

MORRIS. [*Splitting the silence on a high unnatural note.*] Wait a bit! Wait a bit! I've got you! I'll have you!... [*He strides wildly up and down the room, biting his finger.*] You put a wire ... no, that can't be it....

DOCTOR. [*Speaking to him soothingly.*] Well, well, just at this moment we need not inquire....

MORRIS. [*Turning on him furiously.*] You call yourself a man of science, and you dare to tell me not to inquire!

SMITH. We only mean that for the moment you might let it alone.

MORRIS. [*Violently.*] No, Priest, I will not let it alone. [*Pacing the room again.*] Could it be done with mirrors? [*He clasps his brow.*] You have a mirror.... [*Suddenly, with a shout.*] I've got it! I've got it! Mixture of lights! Why not? If you throw a green light on a red light....

[*Sudden silence.*

SMITH. [*Quietly to the* Doctor.] You don't get blue.

DOCTOR. [*Stepping across to the* Conjurer.] If you have done this trick, for God's sake undo it.

[*After a silence, the light turns red again.*

MORRIS. [*Dashing suddenly to the glass doors and examining them.*] It's the glass! You've been doing something to the glass!

[*He stops suddenly and there is a long silence.*

CONJURER. [*Still without moving.*] I don't think you will find anything wrong with the glass.

MORRIS. [*Bursting open the glass doors with a crash.*] Then I'll find out what's wrong with the lamp.

[*Disappears into the garden.*

DOCTOR. It is still a wet night, I am afraid.

SMITH. Yes. And somebody else will be wandering about the garden now.

[*Through the broken glass doors* Morris *can be seen marching backwards and forwards with swifter and swifter steps.*

SMITH. I suppose in this case the Celtic twilight will not get on the chest.

DOCTOR. Oh, if it were only the chest!

Enter Patricia.

PATRICIA. Where is my brother?

[*There is an embarrassed silence, in which the* Conjurer *answers.*

CONJURER. I am afraid he is walking about in Fairyland.

PATRICIA. But he mustn't go out on a night like this; it's very dangerous!

CONJURER. Yes, it is very dangerous. He might meet a fairy.

PATRICIA. What do you mean?

CONJURER. You went out in this sort of weather and you met this sort of fairy, and so far it has only brought you sorrow.

PATRICIA. I am going out to find my brother.

[*She goes out into the garden through the open doors.*

SMITH. [*After a silence, very suddenly.*] What is that noise? She is not singing those songs to him, is she?

CONJURER. No. He does not understand the language of the elves.

47

SMITH. But what are all those cries and gasps I hear?

CONJURER. The normal noises, I believe, of a quiet business man.

DOCTOR. Sir, I can understand your being bitter, for I admit you have been uncivilly received; but to speak like that just now....

[Patricia *reappears at the garden doors, very pale.*

PATRICIA. Can I speak to the Doctor?

DOCTOR. My dear lady, certainly. Shall I fetch the Duke?

PATRICIA. I would prefer the Doctor.

SMITH. Can I be of any use?

PATRICIA. I only want the Doctor.

[*Quietly.*] That last was a wonderful trick of yours.

SMITH. [*Quietly.*] That last was a wonderful trick of yours.

CONJURER. Thank you. I suppose you mean it was the only one you didn't see through.

SMITH. Something of the kind, I confess. Your last trick was the best trick I have ever seen. It is so good that I wish you had not done it.

CONJURER. And so do I.

SMITH. How do you mean? Do you wish you had never been a conjurer?

CONJURER. I wish I had never been born.

[*Exit* Conjurer.

[*A silence. The* Doctor *enters, very grave.*

DOCTOR. It is all right so far. We have brought him back.

SMITH. [*Drawing near to him.*] You told me there was mental trouble with the girl.

DOCTOR. [*Looking at him steadily.*] No. I told you *there was mental trouble in the family.*

SMITH. [*After a silence.*] Where is Mr. Morris Carleon?

DOCTOR. I have got him into bed in the next room. His sister is looking after him.

SMITH. His sister! Oh, then do you believe in fairies?

DOCTOR. Believe in fairies? What do you mean?

SMITH. At least you put the person who does believe in them in charge of the person who doesn't.

DOCTOR. Well, I suppose I do.

SMITH. You don't think she'll keep him awake all night with fairy tales?

DOCTOR. Certainly not.

SMITH. You don't think she'll throw the medicine-bottle out of window and administer—er—a dewdrop, or anything of that sort? Or a four-leaved clover, say?

DOCTOR. No; of course not.

SMITH. I only ask because you scientific men are a little hard on us clergymen. You don't believe in a priesthood; but you'll admit I'm more really a priest than this Conjurer is really a magician. You've been talking a lot about the Bible and the Higher Criticism.

49

But even by the Higher Criticism the Bible is older than the language of the elves—which was, as far as I can make out, invented this afternoon. But Miss Carleon believed in the wizard. Miss Carleon believed in the language of the elves. And you put her in charge of an invalid without a flicker of doubt: because you trust women.

DOCTOR. [*Very seriously.*] Yes, I trust women.

SMITH. You trust a woman with the practical issues of life and death, through sleepless hours when a shaking hand or an extra grain would kill.

DOCTOR. Yes.

SMITH. But if the woman gets up to go to early service at my church, you call her weak-minded and say that nobody but women can believe in religion.

DOCTOR. I should never call this woman weak-minded—no, by God, not even if she went to church.

SMITH. Yet there are many as strong-minded who believe passionately in going to church.

DOCTOR. Weren't there as many who believed passionately in Apollo?

SMITH. And what harm came of believing in Apollo? And what a mass of harm may have come of not believing in Apollo? Does it never strike you that doubt can be a madness, as well be faith? That asking questions may be a disease, as well as proclaiming doctrines? You talk of religious mania! Is there no such thing as irreligious mania? Is there no such thing in the house at this moment?

DOCTOR. Then you think no one should question at all.

SMITH. [*With passion, pointing to the next room.*] I think that is what comes of questioning! Why can't you leave the universe alone and let it mean what it likes? Why shouldn't the thunder be Jupiter? More men have made themselves silly by wondering what the devil it was if it wasn't Jupiter.

DOCTOR. [*Looking at him.*] Do you believe in your own religion?

SMITH. [*Returning the look equally steadily.*] Suppose I don't: I should still be a fool to question it. The child who doubts about Santa Claus has insomnia. The child who believes has a good night's rest.

DOCTOR. You are a Pragmatist.

Enter Duke, *absent-mindedly.*

SMITH. That is what the lawyers call vulgar abuse. But I do appeal to practise. Here is a family over which you tell me a mental calamity hovers. Here is the boy who questions everything and a girl who can believe anything. Upon which has the curse fallen?

DUKE. Talking about the Pragmatists. I'm glad to hear.... Ah, very forward movement! I suppose Roosevelt now.... [*Silence.*] Well, we move you know, we move! First there was the Missing Link. [*Silence.*] No! First there was Protoplasm—and then there was the Missing Link; and Magna Carta and so on. [*Silence.*] Why, look at the Insurance Act!

DOCTOR. I would rather not.

DUKE. [*Wagging a playful finger at him.*] Ah, prejudice, prejudice! You doctors, you know! Well, I never had any myself. [*Silence.*

DOCTOR. [*Breaking the silence in unusual*

exasperation.] Any what?

DUKE. [*Firmly.*] Never had any Marconis myself. Wouldn't touch 'em. [*Silence.*] Well, I must speak to Hastings.

[*Exit Duke, aimlessly.*

DOCTOR. [*Exploding.*] Well, of all the.... [*Turns to Smith.*] You asked me just now which member of the family had inherited the family madness.

SMITH. Yes; I did.

DOCTOR. [*In a low, emphatic voice.*] On my living soul, I believe it must be the Duke.

CURTAIN

ACT III

Room partly darkened, a table with a lamp on it, and an empty chair. From room next door faint and occasional sounds of the tossing or talking of the invalid.

Enter Doctor Grimthorpe *with a rather careworn air, and a medicine bottle in his hand. He puts it on the table, and sits down in the chair as if keeping a vigil.*

Enter Conjurer, *carrying his bag, and cloaked for departure. As he crosses the room the* Doctor *rises and calls after him.*

DOCTOR. Forgive me, but may I detain you for one moment? I suppose you are aware that—[*he hesitates*] that there have been rather grave developments in the case of illness which happened after your performance. I would not say, of course, because of your performance.

CONJURER. Thank you.

DOCTOR. [*Slightly encouraged, but speaking very carefully.*] Nevertheless, mental excitement is necessarily an element of importance in physiological troubles, and your triumphs this evening were really so extraordinary that I cannot pretend to dismiss them from my patient's case. He is at present in a state somewhat analogous to delirium, but in which he can still partially ask and answer questions. The question he continually asks is how you managed to do your last trick.

CONJURER. Ah! My last trick!

DOCTOR. Now I was wondering whether we could make any arrangement which would be fair to you in the matter. Would it be possible for you to give me in confidence the means of satisfying this—this fixed idea he seems to have got. [*He hesitates again, and picks his words more slowly.*] This special condition of semi-delirious disputation is a rare one, and connected in my experience with rather unfortunate cases.

CONJURER. [*Looking at him steadily.*] Do you mean he is going mad?

DOCTOR. [*Rather taken aback for the first time.*] Really, you ask me an unfair question. I could not explain the fine shades of these things to a layman. And even if—if what you suggest were so, I should have to regard it as a professional secret.

CONJURER. [*Still looking at him.*] And don't you think you ask me a rather unfair question, Dr. Grimthorpe? If yours is a professional secret, is not mine a professional secret too? If you may hide truth from the world, why may not I? You don't tell your tricks. I don't tell my tricks.

DOCTOR. [*With some heat.*] Ours are not tricks.

CONJURER. [*Reflectively.*] Ah, no one can be sure of that till the tricks are told.

DOCTOR. But the public can see a doctor's cures as plain as....

CONJURER. Yes. As plain as they saw the red lamp over his door this evening.

DOCTOR. [*After a pause.*] Your secret, of course, would be strictly kept by every one involved.

CONJURER. Oh, of course. People in delirium

always keep secrets strictly.

DOCTOR. No one sees the patient but his sister and myself.

CONJURER. [*Starts slightly.*] Yes, his sister. Is she very anxious?

DOCTOR. [*In a lower voice.*] What would you suppose?

[Conjurer *throws himself into the chair, his cloak slipping back from his evening dress. He ruminates for a short space and then speaks.*

CONJURER. Doctor, there are about a thousand reasons why I should not tell you how I really did that trick. But one will suffice, because it is the most practical of all.

DOCTOR. Well? And why shouldn't you tell me?

CONJURER. Because you wouldn't believe me if I did.

[*A silence, the* Doctor *looking at him curiously.*

[*Enter the* Duke *with papers in his hand. His usual gaiety of manner has a rather forced air, owing to the fact that by some vague sick-room associations he walks as if on tip-toe and begins to speak in a sort of loud or shrill whisper. This he fortunately forgets and falls into his more natural voice.*

DUKE. [*To* Conjurer.] So very kind of you to have waited, Professor. I expect Dr. Grimthorpe has explained the little difficulty we are in much better than I could. Nothing like the medical mind for a scientific statement. [*Hazily.*] Look at Ibsen.

[*Silence.*

DOCTOR. Of course the Professor feels considerable reluctance in the matter. He points out that his secrets are an essential part of his profession.

DUKE. Of course, of course. Tricks of the trade, eh? Very proper, of course. Quite a case of noblesse oblige [*Silence.*] But I dare say we shall be able to find a way out of the matter. [*He turns to the* Conjurer.] Now, my dear sir, I hope you will not be offended if I say that this ought to be a business matter. We are asking you for a piece of your professional work and knowledge, and if I may have the pleasure of writing you a cheque....

CONJURER. I thank your Grace, I have already received my cheque from your secretary. You will find it on the counterfoil just after the cheque you so kindly gave to the Society for the Suppression of Conjuring.

DUKE. Now I don't want you to take it in that way. I want you to take it in a broader way. Free, you know. [*With an expansive gesture.*] Modern and all that! Wonderful man, Bernard Shaw!

[*Silence.*

DOCTOR. [*With a slight cough, resuming.*] If you feel any delicacy the payment need not be made merely to you. I quite respect your feelings in the matter.

DUKE. [*Approvingly.*] Quite so, quite so. Haven't you got a Cause or something? Everybody has a cause now, you know. Conjurers' widows or something of that kind.

CONJURER. [*With restraint.*] No; I have no widows.

DUKE. Then something like a pension or annuity

for any widows you may—er—procure. [*Gaily opening his cheque-book and talking slang to show there is no ill-feeling.*] Come, let me call it a couple of thou.

[*The* Conjurer *takes the cheque and looks at it in a grave and doubtful way. As he does so the* Rector *comes slowly into the room.*

CONJURER. You would really be willing to pay a sum like this to know the way I did that trick?

DUKE. I would willingly pay much more.

DOCTOR. I think I explained to you that the case is serious.

CONJURER. [*More and more thoughtful.*] You would pay much more.... [*Suddenly.*] But suppose I tell you the secret and you find there's nothing in it?

DOCTOR. You mean that it's really quite simple? Why, I should say that that would be the best thing that could possibly happen. A little healthy laughter is the best possible thing for convalescence.

CONJURER. [*Still looking gloomily at the cheque.*] I do not think you will laugh.

DUKE. [*Reasoning genially.*] But as you say it is something quite simple.

CONJURER. It is the simplest thing there is in the world. That is why you will not laugh.

DOCTOR. [*Almost nervously.*] Why, what do you mean? What shall we do?

CONJURER. [*Gravely.*] You will disbelieve it.

DOCTOR. And why?

CONJURER. Because it is so simple. [*He springs*

57

suddenly to his feet, the cheque still in his hand.] You ask me how I really did the last trick. I will tell you how I did the last trick. I did it by magic.

[*The* Duke *and* Doctor *stare at him motionless; but the* Rev. Smith *starts and takes a step nearer the table. The* Conjurer *pulls his cloak round his shoulders. This gesture, as of departure, brings the* Doctor *to his feet.*

DOCTOR. [*Astonished and angry.*] Do you really mean that you take the cheque and then tell us it was only magic?

CONJURER. [*Pulling the cheque to pieces.*] I tear the cheque, and I tell you it was only magic.

DOCTOR. [*With violent sincerity.*] But hang it all, there's no such thing.

CONJURER. Yes there is. I wish to God I did not know that there is.

DUKE. [*Rising also.*] Why, really, magic....

CONJURER. [*Contemptuously.*] Yes, your Grace, one of those larger laws you were telling us about.

[*He buttons his cloak up at his throat and takes up his bag. As he does so the* Rev. Smith *steps between him and the door and stops him for a moment.*

SMITH. [*In a low voice.*] One moment, sir.

CONJURER. What do you want?

SMITH. I want to apologize to you. I mean on behalf of the company. I think it was wrong to offer you money. I think it was more wrong to mystify you with medical language and call the thing delirium. I have more respect for conjurer's patter than for doctor's patter. They are both meant to stupify; but yours only to stupify for a moment. Now I put it to you in plain words and on plain human Christian grounds. Here is a poor boy who may be going mad. Suppose you had a son in such a position, would you not expect people to tell you the whole truth if it could help you?

CONJURER. Yes. And I have told you the whole truth. Go and find out if it helps you.

[*Turns again to go, but more irresolutely.*

SMITH. You know quite well it will not help us.

CONJURER. Why not?

SMITH. You know quite well why not. You are an honest man; and you have said it yourself. Because he would not believe it.

CONJURER. [*With a sort of fury.*] Well, does anybody believe it? Do you believe it?

SMITH. [*With great restraint.*] Your question is quite fair. Come, let us sit down and talk about it. Let me take your cloak.

CONJURER. I will take off my cloak when you take off your coat.

SMITH. [*Smiling.*] Why? Do you want me to fight?

CONJURER. [*Violently.*] I want you to be martyred. I want you to bear witness to your own creed. I say these things are supernatural. I say this was done by a spirit. The Doctor does not believe me. He is an agnostic; and he knows everything. The Duke does not believe me; he cannot believe anything so plain as a miracle. But what the devil are you for, if you don't believe in a miracle? What does your coat mean, if it doesn't mean that there is such a thing as the supernatural? What does your cursed collar mean if it doesn't mean that there is such a thing as a spirit? [*Exasperated.*] Why the devil do you dress up like that if you don't believe in it? [*With violence.*] Or perhaps you don't believe in devils?

SMITH. I believe.... [*After a pause.*] I wish I could believe.

CONJURER. Yes. I wish I could disbelieve.

[*Enter* Patricia *pale and in the slight négligée of the amateur nurse.*

PATRICIA. May I speak to the Conjurer?

SMITH. [Hastening *forward.*] You want the Doctor?

PATRICIA. No, the Conjurer.

DOCTOR. Are there any developments?

PATRICIA. I only want to speak to the Conjurer.

[*They all withdraw, either at the garden or the other doors.* Patricia *walks up to* Conjurer.

PATRICIA. You must tell me how you did the trick. You will. I know you will. O, I know my poor brother was rude to you. He's rude to everybody! [*Breaks down.*] But he's such a little, little boy!

CONJURER. I suppose you know there are things men never tell to women. They are too horrible.

PATRICIA. Yes. And there are things women never tell to men. They also are too horrible. I am here to hear them all.

CONJURER. Do you really mean I may say anything I like? However dark it is? However dreadful it is? However damnable it is?

PATRICIA. I have gone through too much to be terrified now. Tell me the very worst.

CONJURER. I will tell you the very worst. I fell in love with you when I first saw you.

[*Sits down and crosses his legs.*

PATRICIA. [*Drawing back.*] You told me I looked like a child and....

CONJURER. I told a lie.

PATRICIA. O; this is terrible.

CONJURER. I was in love, I took an opportunity. You believed quite simply that I was a magician? but I....

PATRICIA. It is terrible. It is terrible. I never believed you were a magician.

CONJURER. [*Astounded.*] Never believed I was a magician...!

PATRICIA. I always knew you were a man.

CONJURER. [*Doing whatever passionate things people do on the stage.*] I am a man. And you are a woman. And all the elves have gone to elfland, and all the devils to hell. And you and I will walk out of this great vulgar house and be married.... Every one is crazy in this house to-night, I think. What am I saying? As if you could marry me! O my God!

PATRICIA. This is the first time you have failed in courage.

CONJURER. What do you mean?

PATRICIA. I mean to draw your attention to the

fact that you have recently made an offer, I accept it.

CONJURER. Oh, it's nonsense, it's nonsense. How can a man marry an archangel, let alone a lady. My mother was a lady and she married a dying fiddler who tramped the roads; and the mixture plays the cat and banjo with my body and soul. I can see my mother now cooking food in dirtier and dirtier lodgings, darning socks with weaker and weaker eyes when she might have worn pearls by consenting to be a rational person.

PATRICIA. And she might have grown pearls, by consenting to be an oyster.

CONJURER. [*Seriously.*] There was little pleasure in her life.

PATRICIA. There is little, a very little, in everybody's. The question is, what kind? We can't turn life into a pleasure. But we can choose such pleasures as are worthy of us and our immortal souls. Your mother chose and I have chosen.

CONJURER. [*Staring.*] Immortal souls!... And I suppose if I knelt down to worship you, you and every one else would laugh.

PATRICIA. [*With a smile of perversity.*] Well, I think this is a more comfortable way. [*She sits down suddenly beside him in a sort of domestic way and goes on talking.*] Yes. I'll do everything your mother did, not so well, of course; I'll darn that conjurer's hat—does one darn hats?—and cook the Conjurer's dinner. By the way, what is a Conjurer's dinner? There's always the goldfish, of course....

CONJURER. [*With a groan.*] Carrots.

PATRICIA. And, of course, now I come to think of

it, you can always take rabbits out of the hat. Why, what a cheap life it must be! How do you cook rabbits? The Duke is always talking about poached rabbits. Really, we shall be as happy as is good for us. We'll have confidence in each other at least, and no secrets. I insist on knowing all the tricks.

CONJURER. I don't think I know whether I'm on my head or my heels.

PATRICIA. And now, as we're going to be so confidential and comfortable, you'll just tell me the real, practical, tricky little way you did that last trick.

CONJURER. [*Rising, rigid with horror.*] How I did that trick? I did it by devils. [*Turning furiously on Patricia.*] You could believe in fairies. Can't you believe in devils?

PATRICIA. [*Seriously.*] No, I can't believe in devils.

CONJURER. Well, this room is full of them.

PATRICIA. What does it all mean?

CONJURER. It only means that I have done what many men have done; but few, I think, have thriven by. [*He sits down and talks thoughtfully.*] I told you I had mixed with many queer sets of people. Among others, I mixed with those who pretend, truly and falsely, to do our tricks by the aid of spirits. I dabbled a little in table-rapping and table-turning. But I soon had reason to give it up.

PATRICIA. Why did you give it up?

CONJURER. It began by giving me headaches. And I found that every morning after a Spiritualist séance I had a queer feeling of lowness and degradation, of having been soiled; much like the feeling, I suppose, that people have the morning after they have been drunk. But I happen to have what people call a strong head; and I have never been really drunk.

PATRICIA. I am glad of that.

CONJURER. It hasn't been for want of trying. But it wasn't long before the spirits with whom I had been playing at table-turning, did what I think they generally do at the end of all such table-turning.

PATRICIA. What did they do?

CONJURER. They turned the tables. They turned the tables upon me. I don't wonder at your believing in fairies. As long as these things were my servants they seemed to me like fairies. When they tried to be my masters.... I found they were not fairies. I found the spirits with whom I at least had come in contact were evil ... awfully, unnaturally evil.

PATRICIA. Did they say so?

CONJURER. Don't talk of what they said. I was a loose fellow, but I had not fallen so low as such things. I resisted them; and after a pretty bad time, psychologically speaking, I cut the connexion. But they were always tempting me to use the supernatural power I had got from them. It was not very great, but it was enough to move things about, to alter lights, and so on. I don't know whether you realize that it's rather a strain on a man to drink bad coffee at a coffee-stall when he knows he has just enough magic in him to make a bottle of champagne walk out of an empty shop.

PATRICIA. I think you behaved very well.

CONJURER. [*Bitterly.*] And when I fell at last it was for nothing half so clean and Christian as champagne. In black blind pride and anger and all kinds of heathenry, because of the impudence of a schoolboy, I called on the fiends and they obeyed.

PATRICIA. [*Touches his arm.*] Poor fellow!

CONJURER. Your goodness is the only goodness that never goes wrong.

PATRICIA. And what are we to do with Morris? I—I believe you now, my dear. But he—he will never believe.

CONJURER. There is no bigot like the atheist. I must think.

[*Walks towards the garden windows. The other men reappear to arrest his movement.*

DOCTOR. Where are you going?

CONJURER. I am going to ask the God whose enemies I have served if I am still worthy to save a child.

[*Exit into garden. He paces up and down exactly as* Morris *has done. As he does so,* Patricia *slowly goes out; and a long silence follows, during which the remaining men stir and stamp very restlessly. The darkness increases. It is long before anyone speaks.*

DOCTOR. [*Abruptly.*] Remarkable man that Conjurer. Clever man. Curious man. Very curious man. A kind of man, you know.... Lord bless us! What's that?

DUKE. What's what, eh? What's what?

DOCTOR. I swear I heard a footstep.

Enter Hastings *with papers.*

DUKE. Why, Hastings—Hastings—we thought you were a ghost. You must be—er—looking white or something.

HASTINGS. I have brought back the answer of the Anti-Vegetarians ... I mean the Vegetarians.

[*Drops one or two papers.*

DUKE. Why, Hastings, you are looking white.

HASTINGS. I ask your Grace's pardon. I had a slight shock on entering the room.

DOCTOR. A shock? What shock?

HASTINGS. It is the first time, I think, that your Grace's work has been disturbed by any private feelings of mine. I shall not trouble your Grace with them. It will not occur again.

[*Exit Hastings.*

DUKE. What an extraordinary fellow. I wonder if....

[*Suddenly stops speaking.*

DOCTOR. [*After a long silence, in a low voice to* Smith.] How do you feel?

SMITH. I feel I must have a window shut or I must have it open, and I don't know which it is.

[*Another long silence.*

SMITH. [*Crying out suddenly in the dark.*] In God's name, go!

DOCTOR. [*Jumping up rather in a tremble.*] Really, sir, I am not used to being spoken to....

SMITH. It was not you whom I told to go.

DOCTOR. No. [*Pause.*] But I think I will go. This room is simply horrible.

[*He marches towards the door.*

DUKE. [*Jumping up and bustling about, altering cards, papers, etc., on tables.*] Room horrible? Room horrible? No, no, no. [*Begins to run quicker round the room, flapping his hands like fins.*] Only a little crowded. A little crowded. And I don't seem to know all the people. We can't like everybody. These large at-homes....

[*Tumbles on to a chair.*

CONJURER. [*Reappearing at the garden doors.*] Go back to hell from which I called you. It is the last order I shall give.

DOCTOR. [*Rising rather shakily.*] And what are you going to do?

CONJURER. I am going to tell that poor little lad a lie. I have found in the garden what he did not find in the garden. I have managed to think of a natural explanation of that trick.

DOCTOR. [*Warmly moved.*] I think you are something like a great man. Can I take your explanation to him now?

CONJURER. [*Grimly.*] No thank you. I will take it myself.

[*Exit into the other room.*

DUKE. [*Uneasily.*] We all felt devilish queer just now. Wonderful things there are in the world. [*After a pause.*] I suppose it's all electricity.

[*Silence as usual.*

SMITH. I think there has been more than electricity in all this.

Enter Patricia, *still pale, but radiant.*

PATRICIA. Oh, Morris is ever so much better! The Conjurer has told him such a good story of how the trick was done.

Enter Conjurer.

DUKE. Professor, we owe you a thousand thanks!

DOCTOR. Really, you have doubled your claim to originality!

SMITH. It is much more marvellous to explain a miracle than to work a miracle. What was your explanation, by the way?

CONJURER. I shall not tell you.

SMITH. [*Starting.*] Indeed? Why not?

CONJURER. Because God and the demons and that Immortal Mystery that you deny has been in this room to-night. Because you know it has been here. Because you have felt it here. Because you know the spirits as well as I do and fear them as much as I do.

SMITH. Well?

CONJURER. Because all this would not avail. If I told you the lie I told Morris Carleon about how I did that trick....

SMITH. Well?

CONJURER. You would believe it as he believed it. You cannot think [*pointing to the lamp*] how that trick could be done naturally. I alone found out how it

68

could be done—after I had done it by magic. But if I tell you a natural way of doing it....

SMITH. Well?...

CONJURER. Half an hour after I have left this house you will be all saying how it was done.

[Conjurer *buttons up his cloak and advances to* Patricia.

CONJURER. Good-bye.

PATRICIA. I shall not say good-bye.

CONJURER. You are great as well as good. But a saint can be a temptress as well as a sinner. I put my honour in your hands ... oh, yes, I have a little left. We began with a fairy tale. Have I any right to take advantage of that fairy tale? Has not that fairy tale really and truly come to an end?

PATRICIA. Yes. That fairy tale has really and truly come to an end. [*Looks at him a little in the old mystical manner.*] It is very hard for a fairy tale to come to an end. If you leave it alone it lingers everlastingly. Our fairy tale has come to an end in the only way a fairy tale can come to an end. The only way a fairy tale can leave off being a fairy tale.

CONJURER. I don't understand you.

PATRICIA. It has come true.

CURTAIN